No More Settling

Finding Wholeness in Relationships

Latoya S. Kight

Contents

INTRODUCTION i

SECTION 1: FAMILY 1

    Chapter 1. Parent/Child 3
    Chapter 2. Siblings 21
    Chapter 3. Fighting For Each Other 27

SECTION TWO: FRIENDSHIP 29

    Chapter 4. Meeting And Connecting 31
    Chapter 5. Learning Each Other 35
    Chapter 6. Learning From Each Other 41
    Chapter 7. Seasonal/Failed Friendships 45

SECTION THREE: DATING/MARRIAGE 49

    Chapter 8.   Self-Love 51
    Chapter 9.   Setting Standards 57
    Chapter 10. Surviving Breakups/Divorce 63
    Chapter 11. Recognizing True Love 71
    Chapter 12. Happily Ever After 79
    Chapter 13. Learning Your Mate 83

CONCLUSION 89

INTRODUCTION

My life has been FULL of ups and downs. This thing called life will throw a curveball at you, and my life has been FULL of curveballs: curveballs I couldn't have anticipated or have been prepared for. If you think you're prepared, then you've got another thing coming.

When you are born you can't imagine all the problems you will face. You definitely don't ask for it. Who wants turmoil? Not me. There's no way I wanted to be born to a teenage mom. I couldn't have possibly asked to be raised without my real dad. I definitely didn't desire to grow up in a home full of people and still feel lonely. I didn't want to become pregnant at the age of 16. I surely didn't want to become pregnant again at 17. I never asked to be in a tumultuous marriage. My dream didn't include a divorce. On top of it all, I suffered from mental and emotional abuse, heartache, pain, rejection, low self-esteem, and stress. This was not what I wanted for my life or what I prayed for. However, continued prayer and reflection made me realize that the key to my happiness was making sure all of my relationships were healthy, and that journey would have to start with being healthy myself. After this realization, my life completely turned around.

There's no need to live life lonely, angry, and damaged; you were not created to suffer. Our Creator built us to be happy and healthy. Granted, obtaining healthy relationships takes a lot of work and keeping them requires even more energy and perseverance. So, you have to be willing to change, give up unhealthy tendencies, and compromise. If you are willing to brave these challenges and look inside yourself, you will find all the nasty mess that you've buried as excuses and self-bashing that you need to remove. These are your hidden wounds, hurts that never healed, and issues you never confronted that you'll have to confront and resolve before you can have the healthy relationships that help make you whole. Friends and family are some of the greatest gifts God has given us. Don't miss out on the beauty of it all due to your own selfish motives.

My happiness and wellbeing largely depended on learning how to achieve and maintain strong and healthy relationships: as a daughter, sister, mother, wife, friend, niece, granddaughter, and cousin. I wanted to be able to have relationships with my family and friends that not only brought out the best in myself but in them as well. This meant establishing a meaningful connection beyond mere titles. Whether we succeeded or failed at our attempt, I wanted to enjoy growing together knowing that we at least tried.

Not all of my relationships have been perfect, but I tapped into something years ago that helped me view and treat my relationships differently. When I realized the people around me were my allies, not my enemies, I changed how I treated them. I knew I needed these relationships to survive so I began to show my appreciation for the people in my life more. If I wanted to be respected, I needed to be respectful in turn. I craved connections that were valuable to everyone involved. I wanted to be spoken well of and vice versa. I desired to give and not just receive. I wanted to make a positive impact on everyone around me.

I wrote this book to highlight some of the lessons I have learned on my journey, which have allowed me to grow tremendously. I'm finally experiencing a more fulfilling and healthy life because my relationships are stronger; they are connections I and loved ones can turn to for inspiration and guidance. This is a goal I never believed was possible. "There's no way that someone could be happy with all their relationships," I once thought. Well, I'm here to let you know that's a lie. You CAN have and nurture relationships that are empowering, healthy, and whole.

SECTION ONE:
FAMILY

Chapter 1: Parent/Child

Parents and caregivers are the first to bond with their child: they are the child's first teachers, role models, friends, and examples of what it means to be in a healthy (or unhealthy) relationship. When a parent decides they are going to bring another life into this world, they have to start making decisions as if the child is already here. Most parents make significant lifestyle changes like hanging out late or with the wrong crowd. They'd rather stay home than go club hopping. Most parents change their spending habits. Some start making room for the child by changing vehicles and homes. Others prepare the people in their life for their child because they want to make sure that the child is surrounded by people that care and love them.

Parenting doesn't come with a handbook. While there are books out there to help you with what to expect when you become a parent, there isn't a single one that can prepare you for the unpredictability of parenthood. No book could tell me how to deal with four children with different personalities. They couldn't tell me how to raise healthy kids when I was just a child myself. Books couldn't show me how to confront my depression while making sure my children weren't affected. It wouldn't be able to warn me that my children would have their own issues and how to help my children work through them. I had to figure it out along the way with God on my side.

Perfection is not a part of becoming happy, healthy, and whole as a family. No family is the same, and it's what you do with what you've got that counts. There are single parents, married parents, and blended families. Depending on the makeup of your family, how you raise your child changes.

My mom wasn't prepared to be a parent: she had me at a very young age and had to leave my biological father because he was abusive. Raising a child was tough for my mom on top of dealing with a man that didn't respect her. It's a lot for a young mother to deal with alone. My stepfather, who raised me with my mom, was the only father-figure I knew until I became a teenager.

My mom and my stepfather were strict with me. They didn't allow me to get involved in most of the activities other kids my age were allowed to do so I would avoid trouble. While kids my age were able to hang out and party I didn't get to. I couldn't go to just anyone's house. I wasn't allowed to watch or listen to shows that were inappropriate. It was important to my parents that I was raised as a Christian and with all the values of morality and proper behavior that included. I went to church constantly and was taught to respect both adults and God. My mother was my example of a good Christian, portraying the Godly woman at all times and in all aspects of her life. At the time, I was not happy with the lack of freedom I had during my teen years, but as time went on, I understood the benefits of leading a Godly life.

I would describe my early relationship with my mom and stepfather as unbalanced. My mom and I didn't fight much, but she worked a lot, so I didn't get to spend much of quality time with her. I always wanted more from our relationship, and she did the best she could, but she simply didn't have the time to foster the bond that I desired. My stepfather and I didn't click much. Even though he lived in the house, he never felt present. We didn't really have heart-to-heart moments and quality time was nonexistent for the most part. I longed to bond with both my mom and my stepfather, a bond that went beyond merely providing for me.

Occasionally, my mom and stepfather took my siblings and I on vacations. I always looked forward to these yearly trips because it was a rare time when the family was all together. Instead of the normal "go-your-separate-ways" mentality that normally controlled our daily lives, our family would get to spend quality time together away from home. Those trips allowed me to see a different side of both my mom and my stepfather. Instead of the distant parent that was constantly working, I saw that they both could be fun and loving people. They truly cared for and wanted to make time for us. As you read about relationships in this book, keep in mind that caring for and making time for your family, even when it seems impossible, is everything.

When I was about 17 years old, I discovered that my stepfather wasn't my biological father. Deep down, I think I always knew, but I wanted to believe that my parents would be upfront with me about the identity of my real dad. Since neither my mom nor my stepfather told me anything, I assumed that there was nothing to tell. I was upset with my mom for not telling me about my biological father; I felt that her keeping my real dad away from me was selfish. Who gave her this right to choose my father? However, I was also excited: now, I could have the father I always wanted. There was no way my real dad would be anything less than a real-life Superman: I imagined him as loving, caring, protective, and kind. I thought, "Finally! Now I can be completely happy." I couldn't have been more wrong. He was the TOTAL opposite! He was mean, controlling, and unpleasant, and even though I tried to create a bond with him, we never saw eye-to-eye. He was always defensive, and his way of thinking was always negative. Before I knew that he was my biological father, he told me that he tried to get in contact with me, but my mom wouldn't let it happen. Even if what he said was true, I felt that he could have done more to be a positive presence in my life, but he didn't. I tried everything to make the relationship with my real father work. I would call him, and he would visit, but he was so difficult to deal with. He also became a bad influence in my life. Despite my strict upbringing before I met him, I started making bad decisions.

My mom raised me with a sense of strong moral values, but I was still missing something from my life. I often felt unloved and unwanted by everyone around me. There were times I wanted to run away or kill myself. However, I suffered in silence: neither my parents nor my siblings knew how alone I felt. It was hard sharing my feelings with anyone because I didn't think anyone would respect them. With my mom working so much, I didn't feel like I could talk to her, and I definitely didn't talk to my step-dad because he just seemed emotionally unavailable. The absence of communication can leave a person to think anything. A lot gets conjured up and misconstrued when you don't have honest conversation. I felt that I needed to fill this void in my life, so I became pregnant at the young age of 16.

My pregnancy was planned. I felt alone and wanted to have a child, so she would love me, and I would love her in return: an open and reciprocal relationship

I felt I was not getting from my mom, my step-dad, or my biological father. However, when my mom found out I was pregnant, it put a deep strain on our already tension-filled relationship. She was extremely disappointed and upset with me: I was entirely too young to be a mother, and she better than anyone knew that it was not easy to raise a child when you're only a child yourself. She was hurt by my decision more than I could imagine. She was never a sensitive woman and did not show her feelings easily. It hurt me deeply to see her so distressed by my mistake. All children want is for their parents to be proud of them, so watching my mom try to process this next phase of my life was eye opening. I suddenly realized I had my mom all wrong. I thought she didn't care much. I believed that she was emotionless. It never occurred to me that my mother was a human being like me. That's the moment I knew that parents and children both deal with issues. Adults have feelings too, but when they're hidden from their child, the child grows up believing their parents are superheroes and nothing can touch them. Man, was I wrong!

    Even though my mom didn't want to deal with me and my pregnancy in the beginning, she came around later and was a supportive and loving grandmother to her granddaughter. She may not have been proud of me, but she never made my daughter feel like a mistake. Watching my mother with my daughter made me wonder why I never had the caring relationship with my mother that she seemed willing to share with her granddaughter but not with me. As I watched my mom and my daughter, I saw my mom in a different light. My mom adored my daughter and always bragged about her. My mom's face would light up whenever she spent time with her. My mom spoiled my daughter heavily, so she was never without her grandmother's devotion and love. I am in awe of their bond and love that my daughter has a great relationship with her grandmother.

My parents made sure that my daughter's father and I took responsibility for our actions: we both had to work and make sure we graduated high school. However, by the time I graduated, I was pregnant with our second child. I tried to keep my second pregnancy a secret, but eventually my parents found out. My mom and I had a big fight. Even though I don't remember exactly what was said, I know it was so bad that I quickly moved out because I knew she was going to lose it with me. I was so hurt and wanted nothing to do with my parents. After I left their house, I didn't talk to either my mom or my step-dad much.

By the time my second daughter was born, my mom and I were on speaking terms again, and we slowly started rebuilding our relationship. My stepfather wasn't really in the picture anymore due to their divorce, so I was able to bond with my mom in a way that we never had the opportunity to when she was still married to my stepfather. My mom and I's shared love for my kids strengthened our relationship: I began to understand what a struggle it was for my mom to raise kids, and my heart opened up to her. The more I raised my kids the more I understood and became grateful for the way my mother raised me. I constantly apologize to my mom for how I treated her and make sure I let her know how appreciated she is to me now.

I may have had my kids young, but I wasn't out of control. The standards and morals that my mom instilled in me stayed with me. No matter what I went through, her voice would always be in the back of mind. I never wanted to do anything to embarrass her. My mom's opinion of me still holds a lot of weight in my life, and I desire still to be someone my mother can be proud of and admire.

My mom made the best decision she could for me by deciding to keep me away from my biological father. I am so grateful to her for taking full responsibility for raising me and not allowing him to influence my upbringing. She never once said anything negative or hurtful against him, even though she could have, which allowed me to make my own decisions about what kind of parent my father was. Through her strength, my mom showed me how to be a woman of honor even if you have been wronged or are hurt.

Getting to know my biological father also made me appreciate my stepfather: he stepped in to raise a child that wasn't his even though he had no obligation to me. I could have been without a father-figure when I was a child but because of his decision to help my mom raise me, I was raised by two parents instead of one. It took me going down the wrong path to realize the sacrifices my parents made for me and how much their protection meant to me.

Although I had two kids at a young age, I still wanted to please the people around me. I felt I had to make up for my mistakes. It goes to show how vital it is to have a healthy relationship with the man raising you or your father. It can overshadow all the goodness in you to cause you to make unhealthy decisions. The low self-esteem and poor confidence you develop can be so crippling to your character that you lose your self-worth. You don't believe that anyone can love you because you don't love yourself. You can't fathom someone believing you're pretty when you don't hear it or see it. It's so important that children know they are loved, supported, and cared about so they can have the opportunity to be the best versions of themselves.

My husband and I constantly communicate with our children to make sure they know how valuable they are to us and to the world. Our goal is to raise respectful, integrity-filled, wise, intelligent, and successful children. You must guide children on the right path until they are able to venture out on their own. I'm not a "do as I say, not as I do" parent. No matter how much parents feel we're adults that should be able to do and say whatever we want, we must be mindful of the fact that our children are always looking to us and observing our actions. They will always be more prone to do what they see others doing, so as parents, we must be positive examples for our children. It is our duty to mold and shape them into kind and responsible people. Since our children are so susceptible to the influence of their environment, it's important that we understand and respect that kids comprehend the world differently. We must teach them right and wrong by showing them; not just saying it. The toxic habits we keep shouldn't be displayed in front of our kids.

Set standards for your children at a young age. Some parents may feel that kids don't need rules when they're young. However, when a child has structure in their lives, they are more likely to behave properly. Set non-negotiables as they get older. Give them guidelines to adhere to and consequences for not meeting them. Kids respond well to consistency and they don't take well to flakiness. There must be a clear awareness of who is in charge and what is expected of them.

You don't want the world to set the tone for your children on what to be and how to act: they need that foundation from you. Watching other kids misbehave, I wanted to make sure my children weren't "problem children". Parents always have to keep in mind that we are not the only people our children interact with, and everyone isn't as patient as we are. Start teaching your children early how to conduct themselves in public as well as at home. You can't expect a child to automatically know how to behave when you are away from home. You must make your expectations known at all times.

As a parent, you must not only be mindful of what you do or say around your children but what you *don't* say. Most of my experience during my childhood and adolescence was that families didn't talk much. The things that were unsaid led me to believe no one cared. It caused me to make the decision to become pregnant young. I was lost. I felt alone. I didn't know that my mom was doing all she could to give me a good life. I was too busy looking at what I didn't have. I just wanted to feel understood and like I mattered. However, having my own family taught me how to communicate with my children so they never had to experience the hole I felt during my childhood and adolescence.

I always try to lead a life that in no way embarrasses my family. I always think of how my actions will affect them before I make a decision. I always want my children to see a healthy and functional woman when they look at their mother. I refuse to say and do a lot that can be considered damaging to my reputation: not only to be pleasing to God but to make sure my kids understand that you can lead a life that is respectable. By example, I desire to show my daughters the type of women they should be and show my son the type of women he should admire.

I always want my kids to be able to talk to me about anything. I try to make our home an open and safe environment for them to express themselves. It's vital that children feel safe when talking to their parents. You don't want them to entrust their deepest issues or feelings with anyone outside of you. It doesn't hurt for them to talk to others but usually it's best for parents to be their children's go-to people when it comes to important discussions, such as sex, drugs, alcohol, relationships, anger, depression, etc. Not everyone has their best interests in mind, and for these pivotal issues, you want to have the opportunity to guide your child in the right direction. With negative influences and bad advice, they can easily be lead down a bad path. The lack of good advice I received or didn't accept caused me to make horrible decisions. I looked for my answers in a bottle, partying, and men. There was a hole no one ever helped me fill so I tried to fill it myself.

When my biological dad died, I was devastated. In my mind, no matter how hard I tried to have a great relationship with him, the opportunity of having a father that was present in my life, both mentally and physically, died with him. I felt like I was robbed of having a father/daughter bond, and it seemed as if I wasn't meant to have a stand-up father. As a teen, I started connecting myself with positive and upstanding men. I figured if the ones that were supposed to play that role didn't step up, I would create my own healthy father/daughter bonds with men that would show me how children and women should be loved. I was determined to have what I missed out on. I refused to live life never knowing the fulfillment of having the father/daughter bond I craved. There was no way I wouldn't get what I felt I deserved and I knew I shouldn't accept that this was how my life should be.

The bond between a child and a parent plays a huge part in a child's self-esteem. When a child doesn't feel loved or cared for, it can cause that child to look down on themselves. They may feel unwanted and not good enough to receive love. Parents should always make sure their child knows how much they care and how important they are to them. A child should never be hurt by a parent in any way. Parents need to shape and mold their children into who they are meant to be: happy, healthy, and whole. No parent is perfect, but it is your duty to your children to ensure that you do everything in your power to make your child feel secure. They may not show it, but kids don't care about how much money you spend on them but how present you are in their life. Quality time is essential to their well-being. It may seem like presence only has minor influence but to a child it's a huge aspect in their confidence and a gift they'll remember for a lifetime.

Children can be hard to figure out. As a parent, there will be times that you'll feel you aren't raising your children right no matter how much you discipline, instruct, love, support, and take care of them. There will always be some part of you that wonders if you are putting your kids on the right track. However, you can't shift your standards as a parent to appease them. Sometimes they won't like you. There are going to be times they won't understand you or see you in a positive light or you won't understand them. They will challenge you and push you to the limit of your patience, but you must always have the upper hand. Remember, you're the adult.

Being a parent comes with the responsibility of making tough decisions. It also comes with harsh realities that these human beings you've created and take care of won't always make you proud. Kids can be insensitive, selfish, and mean: sometimes it seems they don't believe their actions can affect adults. However, as parents, we must always keep in mind that children deal with a lot that they don't always talk about. So, frustration and pain can come out in unhealthy ways because they don't know how to express themselves. No matter how much you talk to them and try to make them feel important they may resist. Depending on the dynamics of their life, there could be a number of reasons why their actions may seem deliberately hurtful or unfeeling.

Don't beat yourself up over some of the things your children do or say. Kids act out and, oftentimes, it has nothing to do with you. You *must* stand strong and stick to what you know is right. Pray for guidance and trust God is with them. Don't allow anyone you take care of or raise cause you to lose your mind. Do whatever it takes to help them be amazing human beings. That doesn't mean they will be perfect. As long as you follow God, be reassured that He will direct your path and your child will be all God called them to be.

Chapter 2: Siblings

Brothers and sisters can be the greatest gift that you have in life and your biggest allies. However, if your relationships with your siblings are strained, they can be your worst enemies. Living with other people close in age with you can be very challenging. You all have different approaches, outlooks, and behaviors and cohabitating, whether you're under the same roof or you share a room, can create tension that someone can only understand if they have brothers or sisters.

In my house there were four of us. At times, my relationship with my siblings could be very intense. We fought and argued often. Growing up, we weren't as close as we are now. I always thought it was okay to dislike my sisters and brother as long as we knew, at the end of the day, that we were family. The problem with that idea was it didn't work out too well in practice. Our disdain for each other started to spill over into how we related to each other. We would fight like strangers in the street. I don't think any of us understood, truly, the value of having siblings.

I wasn't close to my sisters or brother and often felt like an outcast. Since I was the oldest, I didn't get as much attention as the others. My brother was so aggravating that I had no desire to be close to him. He didn't exemplify what a brother should've been to me: protective and loving. I later found that he wasn't equipped with the tools to look out for us as much as I thought he should. Most sisters have that brother they can call if another man disrespects them. At the time, my brother wasn't that for me. Instead, I became very close to my god-brother. He always stood up for me. The bullying I experienced lessened when people discovered he was close to me. He taught me how men think. My middle sister didn't live with us for a period of time during our childhood. My most difficult relationship was with her: there was such a contrast between us that it was hard to relate to each other on many levels. We butted heads so much to the point that I gave up on having a bond with her. My baby sister was too young for me to relate to and she was always closer to our middle sister. I always felt left out. For years, I felt like I wasn't the big sister they needed and everything I did seem to never be enough for them. I thought I was ugly, a misfit, weak and an embarrassment to my siblings. It caused me to be nasty and intolerable.

My sisters were popular despite the fact that I was a misfit. I felt like I was liked or tolerated just because I was related to them. I was bullied and talked about so much, I believed there was no way anyone was interested in hanging out with me and kept to myself as much as possible. I didn't know I was depressed, had low self-esteem, and lacked confidence. Because I was hiding these insecurities from myself, my family didn't know I was suffering either. Nothing seemed to fulfill me. Again, it's very important to talk to your children. They could have hidden issues that fester and are ultimately unresolved. I felt I was useless and didn't believe I had a purpose in anyone's life or on earth. As a big sister, I wanted to be closer to my siblings: to be able to communicate with them about our lives and feelings without judgement or negativity.

Once I had my children and moved out, I slowly disconnected myself from my siblings. I started to get used to the idea of not having a relationship with any of them. Eventually, I started to desire a healthy relationship with my siblings. As we matured, we all realized that we needed to do better as brother and sisters. We started to get along and wanted to hang around each other. We began talking more often and spending time with each other, valuing and appreciating one another. I realized that each of us had our individual pain and struggles. We all had different perspectives of our upbringing that led us down different paths. Even though all of us, relatively, had grown up in the same house, we each thought we were the only one hurting. Over time, I came to see my siblings as human beings. Not just people who had lived with me during my childhood. Each of us had feelings and none of us knew how to navigate through them.

Most times, siblings don't know the significance of having each other. The fact that you have an automatic friend in this crazy world is one of God's greatest gifts. You have to understand that your sibling is going to be by your side no matter what. They know the good and bad about you and won't judge you. Your siblings will defend and protect you. I hate that we didn't figure out how important it was for us to have a strong connection until we were older.

Before our relationships could be repaired with each other, we had to decide to forgive each other for any wrongdoings we had caused at each other's hands and own up to our actions. There had to be some serious soul searching done to change how we related to each other. Now that I'm older and have repaired these relationships, I absolutely love having siblings. They have taught me valuable lessons about friendship, loyalty, and commitment.

Chapter 3: Fighting for Each Other

Family isn't always fond of each other. Dysfunction and distance between each other can lead to resentment and jealousy, but you have to make up your mind about what kind of family you want and make it happen. Granted, everyone may not see it your way or always agree, but your desire for encouraging relationships that are healthy and whole should always push you and motivate you to make it work even when it's hard.

Family should always have each other's back. Sadly, this truth can get lost in destructive actions; often, family are the ones that can hurt you the most. Nevertheless, it is important to keep a strong bond between you and your family. Don't only fight for them physically but mentally, emotionally, and spiritually. You want to defend them when it comes to other people and fight to salvage any positive relationship you have. There should never be a time that anyone is able to disrespect or harm someone in your family or that you don't step up to protect a loved one who is being attacked. Don't allow a member of your family to feel alone, especially if you can help by being a pillar of support and a source of comfort. When it comes to showing your family love and loyalty, always use wisdom to guide your actions.

Your family will never be perfect but that's ok. Your goal should always be coming together without arguing and fighting. You should want your family to be enjoyable: when you talk to them, it should be loving and fun, not irritating. Spending time should be a precious pastime not a loathed experience. Seeing each other should make you happy. It should make you feel loved. Family shouldn't be an afterthought. Cherish and love them as much as possible. Do what you can to make everyone see that you will always be there for them. No matter how low they may feel, you want to be there to lift them up.

SECTION TWO: FRIENDSHIP

Chapter 4: Meeting and Connecting

I have found friendship to be one of the most vital relationships in life. Friends can be a listening ear, a shoulder to cry on, and an unbiased voice. Having friends can be an amazing gift: good friends are team players that celebrate who you are as well as encourage you to be the best you can be. Friends in your circle should both support you and call you out when you're not making good decisions.

Sometimes people have a hard time making friends. I've grown up with some of my friends or connected with people by chance, but if you wish to expand your circle, you need to be open to putting yourself out there. If you desire friendships that allow you to be who you are, you have to be willing to be friendly. You can't be unapproachable. Placing yourself in situations to meet others helps you to branch out and meet individuals that not only share your interests but will add diversity and fun to your life. Try church, local and community gatherings, or any location where there is a significant amount of people. It's best to try a place where you go regularly so you're able to get to know people that you've seen regularly but haven't yet taken the time to get to know. I met a lot of my current friends at church, and our relationships have done nothing but flourish from there. If you're lucky, you have strong friendships that have lasted years.

One of my best friends has been my friend since we were about nine. We have been through everything together. Our lives have gone down different paths, but we still ended up together. Growing up we were raised in the same church. We had the same spiritual concepts, and we have been through a lot together. No matter how much we wanted to give up on the friendship, somehow, we never could. We have seen each other through the worst times of our lives and celebrated the greatest times. I can't remember a time we weren't there for each other. She knows all of my secrets. She's one of my most trusted friends. However, not everyone is lucky to have friendships that have lasted through childhood. Sometimes you have to put yourself out there and create friendships as an adult, which can be difficult but just as rewarding. Meeting new people can be scary, but you have to take a chance if you want to build friendships that will last. No one is going to be everything you want them to be.

Feel free to take your time when meeting new people. You won't connect with everyone you meet so you want to make sure that a friendship you decide to be pursue is going to be a valuable one. My main focus when I meet people isn't always friendship. Most of the time I'm just being nice to get through the moment. I don't always expect a lasting relationship. I start talking to them or hanging out with them then we slowly become closer.

Be mindful of the environment you're in when meeting that particular person you feel connected to. People are a product of their environment. So, depending on what path you are on, the person you relate to will either help or hinder you on that path. Link up with people who have somewhat similar interests and are in the position to help you get to another level in your growth.

Develop discernment when dealing with people. If you're patient and you take the time to get to know someone, you won't be caught unaware if they don't meet your expectations. People are not perfect, and they will let you down. Pay close attention; what they do won't take you out because it won't sneak up on you. Watch how they relate to other people and their history of lasting relationships. If they have a bad track record, that's a good indication that they're not going to work it out with you. Friendship, just like any other relationship, shouldn't be taken lightly. If you're not ready to go through highs and lows, thick and thin, then you're not ready to invest in a relationship that makes you your best self. Friends should be able to teach and guide you to be healthier and a better human being. They should be a positive influence. Don't become friends with someone for any reason other than companionship and advancement. You don't want to fill your life with people that will hold you back.

Chapter 5:   Learning Each Other

Getting to know someone can be tough. Most people are guarded at first. If you're checking them out, you can assume they're doing the same to you. If you want to know more about someone, start out with small talk and hang out at places you both like. Slowly reveal things about yourself to each other. If someone trusts you by opening up to you, don't betray that trust. Loyalty is one of the biggest factors of friendships. Stay true to your friends no matter what. They should be able to share some of the deepest parts of themselves with you without fear of their secrets being shared with others. Don't gossip about your friends and don't allow anyone else to. Friends should be able to trust each other at all times and in all scenarios.

Watch how they conduct life. Pay attention to whether their habits are healthy. Listen to what they say. All of these things will help you learn about your friend and decipher whether this will be a long lasting and healthy relationship.

The goal is to have a healthy friendship that withstands anything. You want to have that person that's there through all of the crap that life throws at you: someone who you can cry and vent to about anything. Someone who will get you back in line when you lose your way. Between friends, there has to be respect for each other. You want to create a bond that's tight. This all happens with time.

All of my close friends have been around for years. We learn more and more about each other as time progresses. We fight with and for each other. We stand in the gap for one another. We support each other. We depend on each other. We are loyal. We keep it real at all times. When we recognized the value of our relationships, we made it our business to make sure we protected it. There has been a lot of praying and fighting to protect and keep what we have. Most people never get to experience great friends, so we refuse to lose out on it. Understand that the enemy will come and try to destroy what you have so you will have to be aware and on guard; he comes in ways you wouldn't imagine.

My friends and I have had some challenges that tested the strength of our relationships: some conflicts were big, and some were small but what you learn from all of them is that even the smallest issue can tear up a relationship if you let it. Always remember that you and your friends have different temperaments, lifestyles, and backgrounds that you are trying to bring together to create a bond that is lasting and awesome. It takes time to learn about each other and understanding what you need to do to be a good friend to someone. One of my best friends and I got into a major dispute that could've ended it all. We both are quite stubborn and truly believed that we were justified in how we felt. It took people that cared about us to encourage us to repair our relationship. It took time for my best friend and myself to get back to a good place. We had to work through some painful stuff, but when you have God-ordained friendships, you can't just get rid of them.

You want to be open minded but consistent. You want to be understanding but not passive. Be loving while being firm. Always be real and honest. Let your friends know how you really feel. Communicate so you can come to a mutual understanding.

Respect each other's thoughts and feelings even when you don't agree. Friends have to be comfortable coming to you about anything and everything, so don't allow egos to get in the way. Learn to admit when you're wrong and apologize. After the apology, make efforts to do better. Don't repeat past mistakes even if you feel you didn't do anything wrong. You want that person to always know you care about what they care about. You may not agree with them, but you should definitely respect their decisions. You will clash often: keep in mind that it's momentary. Without all of the information, you don't want to respond to your friend negatively and push them away. Refrain from attacking each other. Words can't be taken back after the heat of the moment. The pain of the situation lingers on when someone feels attacked, so be mindful of what you say and, if necessary, give both yourself and your friend time to breathe before reacting.

Communication is important in all relationships. Your opinion should matter to the ones closest to you and you should value their opinion in turn. At the first sign of an issue, you can't write someone off. Work through the conflict and understand it's okay for the ball to be dropped every now and then. Sometimes the other person will forget something important to you or they won't see why it's important. Don't make it a big issue. Express how it makes you feel and allow them to work on it.

You can't change anyone; you can only meet them as far as they want to progress. If a person is struggling to be a good friend but they are willing to change, you should see evidence over time that that they are willing to grow. The destructive actions they used to do should change. The toxic way they think should become less toxic. Their actions and how they conduct themselves should mature. If you don't see this change then that should let you know this person may not be willing to be the friend that you need. Don't rely on a person's words only. Pay attention to a person's actions to learn about them.

People in your circle should have dreams and goals. They should be working at making their life better and greater because, in turn, their dedication inspires you to do the same. You don't want someone pulling you down because they don't want to improve their lives and you do. Friends should be helping you up, and you all should be working together to get better.

Chapter 6: Learning from Each Other

Every one of my close friends have taught me something that I deem valuable. In some aspect of my life, they have shown me how I can improve or change it. As a mother, sister, daughter, wife, friend, and woman, I have gotten to a healthy place that allows me to have great relationships. A friend without wisdom is useless. A friend that you have to babysit is a waste of time. Friends that you have to constantly take care of can cause aspects of your life to be stagnant and slow. You will look around one day and realize that you haven't gone anywhere. You want to grow daily, and having friends that have been through similar situations to help you navigate is essential to your well-being. Again, this doesn't mean their life is perfect: you can learn from the good and bad in their lives.

However, friends should be an inspiration of courage, perseverance, and victory. But you also have to know where to draw the line between relationships where conflict helps you grow and relationships where conflict brings you down.

All of my friends have different backgrounds and situations. I collect information from each of them: I watch, listen, and ask questions. I don't allow myself to think I know everything. I remind myself that someone always knows more than me, but it doesn't make me a lesser person than they are. That area of expertise just might not be my strongest, so it's wise to learn from someone who has experience. For example, I'm not the best cook; however, one of my best friends is a great cook. I often rely on her to help me out when it comes to making great-tasting meals. I'm not ashamed to ask for her help.

I'm very grateful for all of my friends. It's like God sent a set of people into my life that He knew would benefit me in great ways. My circle sets me straight. When they see me going in the wrong direction, they feel obligated to steer me back to the right path. They don't participate in my pity parties. They make me look at myself instead of blaming things and people for my situations. They give me reality checks and respect my feelings. All of them help me through difficult times: they push and pull me and never let me stay stuck. I'm so appreciative that they have allowed me to have access to their lives and show me different sides and ways of thinking. If your circle doesn't help you to grow, then you don't expose yourself to life and all the beauty it holds. To grow, you must allow your circle of friends to grow with you.

Chapter 7: Seasonal/Failed Friendships

It's tough knowing who will be in your life long term. People seem to have the potential to be around forever, but you will find that is not the case with the majority of the individuals you connect to. Seasonal friends are those people that are around for a period of time and are gone once the purpose of them being in your life is over. This shouldn't end in malice, although some do.

You must have an understanding that everyone isn't meant to stick around for long. Failed friendships are those that just don't work out. You can try as much as you want, and you can hold on as long as you want, but eventually that relationship will die. These relationships are also seasonal, but the difference is that these people were never meant to be in your life long. You try to create a bond then something happens to cause you to not care about or like each other. These types of friendships can have ugly endings. Things are done and said out of hurt and anger that further damage the relationship. You can get to the point where you don't care and start to shut them out. My life has been full of both of these.

I have had friends that I knew would be there until the end of time. Some friendships ended with a mutual understanding that we have grown apart. Other friendships have ended because I wronged them in some way or vice versa. Before I understood the dynamics of relationships, friendships like these used to destroy me and I hated ending relationships, especially friendships.

As I dealt with the removal and disconnection of people, it would send me into emotional turmoil. It made me feel like that little girl that was rejected by most of the people in her life and made me harp on all of my insecurities. I felt I wasn't good enough to be anyone's friend. This also caused me to push people away and put a wall up. I didn't want anyone close enough to see my heart, especially females. I had this view that they were all messy and didn't want to be my friend genuinely. I had to realize that people give me what I give them, and since I was operating out of my insecurities, that's what I received.

My lack of self-esteem hindered me a lot. I couldn't understand why it seemed I could only be close to one of my childhood friends. I would be cool with people, but I didn't have many relationships that stuck, and I felt like I was losing friends all the time. I couldn't understand why people didn't care for me like I did them. I had to do some major self-evaluation to understand why I felt this way, had to shed my insecurities, and change the way I operated as a friend. I had to believe I was good enough to have healthy relationships in my life.

For my actions as a friend to change, I had to become the friend that I desired for myself. I started by getting rid of my misconception that all friends gossip, could not be trusted, turn their backs on you, and don't support each other. My mom is a great example of real friendship. She is a very loyal friend that can be trusted. However, I let the world teach me the opposite. I believed friendship was measured by the length of time the relationship lasted, how much we hung out, and how often we talked. Friendship is so much more than that: it's a commitment. You make a silent vow to be true to another person. It's a marriage without the sexual act. A friend should be set to a standard that no one else is held to with certain expectations in place.

When disrespect and disloyalty come into play, individuals should be called to the table and held accountable for their actions. Friends respect each other no matter what. There should not be a time where offense takes over to the point that you can't rectify a situation. If there is ever a disagreement, remember perception is reality for some people and, often times, there is no way around it. You can only resolve a situation when you are honest about the part you played and are apologetic in turn. The other person must be willing to be honest as well. Don't allow anyone to handcuff you to their feelings. Respect their feelings but don't ever let them keep you bound. Do what you can in your power to make things better. Don't ever be a behind kisser.

SECTION THREE: DATING/MARRIAGE

Chapter 8: Self-Love

Self-love is synonymous with one's own well-being and happiness, parts of myself that I found lacking. I saw myself as unattractive, unpopular, unintelligent, and damaged goods. The unhealthy relationships I had created and surrounded myself with made me feel unworthy. I felt like I was always rejected. I couldn't see much good in myself. Growing up, I only had a few friends that made me feel wanted. No way could I get a good-looking man. The cute boys didn't notice me. I couldn't hang out with the cool girls. They just bullied me.

You must first love yourself to obtain happiness, healthiness, and wholeness in dating and marriage, as with any relationship. You must see yourself as worthy of having companionship and love from someone else. Self-esteem and confidence are key players in any relationship, especially dating and marriage. When you see yourself in a positive manner, it will be easier for you to believe that another person can care about you. It took me years to realize this. I didn't understand that I made choices based on my lack of self-love. My relationship woes opened my eyes to a lot. I kept being hurt and feeling unwanted, so I knew something needed to change about me. I had to tap into the beauty within me before anyone would see the beauty outside of me.

The reason most people are alone is due to their lack of self-love. There is no way you can trust someone to love you if you don't love yourself. Fall in love with yourself before trying to fall in love with someone. The way you treat yourself will be the way you allow someone to treat you. The way you see yourself will be the way someone sees you. Your attitude you have about you will be the same attitude another person will have concerning you. Not everything about you is perfect, but you must love yourself and your imperfections. The way you see yourself will reflect in the way you carry yourself, how you handle your relationships with others, and through your conversations. Your true intentions will be exposed effortlessly, whether you want them to or not. How do you expect someone to love your flaws when you don't love them or aren't aware of all of them?

You would be surprised by how much people are willing to deal with and work with you when they truly love you. Just like you are not perfect neither is the person you will be in a relationship with. Work through your past, and deal with the issues that most don't know you have. Conquer the fears that you have encountered. Overcome the struggles that you have endured. Don't allow the things that you have seen, gone through, or heard cause you to give up on having great relationships. Loving yourself helps you to have hope. It makes you see yourself in a way that no one else may see you yet. It causes others to view you differently, with respect and awe, and you'll notice that the more respect you have for yourself the more others respond positively to your presence. Work on being a better you and love will find you.

Love is an incredible thing when you can view it from an undamaged perspective. You don't have to carry old wounds, scars, and pain into your destined relationship. The unresolved inner issues can destroy something that could change your life for the better. Don't hold onto past pain in an attempt to protect it or use it as a crutch. It will only paralyze you permanently. If you want to know how you really see yourself, pay attention to the thoughts you have when no one is around. Think about how you feel about yourself. Do a self-evaluation. Make an inner pros and cons list. It's very important to know yourself so the opinions of others won't change the way you feel about you. It's so easy to believe and accept the negative, but for the sake of your overall success, you must have a strong and healthy outlook about your inner self. Someone that's interested in you will be attracted to your confidence. Exemplifying toxic characteristics will weigh down a relationship. It will cause the other person to become burdened with always trying to please you and make you happy.

    Your self-esteem can determine if you are willing to push yourself to be great or if you'll wallow in self-pity. Knowing where your self-esteem stems from and what direction it is going can help you handle how it influences your life. Let self-awareness guide you by being honest with yourself and about who you really are. Talk to the people closest to you that are not scared to tell you the truth. It's very important to know yourself as you try to grow and get better. There's no way to be a healthier and better you if you don't do some inner assessments. You can't blame everything and everyone outside of you for whatever you are lacking. You must take responsibility for who and where you are in your life. No one can live your life for you. No matter what anyone else does or what happens it's up to you to believe in who you are.

Chapter 9: Setting Standards

If you want a relationship to be longstanding and healthy, you should have set standards. Setting standards makes clear those non-negotiable actions that you will not participate in or allow the people you desire relationships with to bring to your space. It's the way you know you should be treated. They help filter out people that are not good for you. Your self-esteem helps you establish what your standards are and how they help you to create and maintain healthy relationships.

The level of your self-esteem will direct the path of your relationships. You won't tolerate a lot of things when your self-esteem is where it needs to be. People can't walk over you when you know who you are. No one can treat you less than you deserve when you respect yourself.

When you truly love yourself, there are some things you won't allow another person to do or say to you. You will have confidence enough to believe you deserve better than what they are presenting. This keeps you from staying in unhealthy situations longer than needed. It also helps you to not get involved with someone that doesn't meet your standards. You don't want to get stuck in a relationship that doesn't fulfill you the majority of the time.

If you get stuck in an unhealthy relationship, it will cause you to become bitter and resent your mate. I settled for relationships in the past that didn't benefit myself or the other people just to not be alone. They were destined for disaster because they were not God-ordained.

Don't get caught up in believing that standards make you stuck up or picky. Honestly, the point is to be picky. You don't want to be in relationship with just anybody and you don't want to waste time with someone thinking they are the one and they turn out to be a disappointment. Being around someone constantly and having disdain for them is never healthy. The goal is to have a God-ordained, healthy relationship. Seek God's advice on whether your standards are sensible and reachable. It's okay to compromise with the understanding that you won't get everything you want but you should get as close to it as possible. Your desires are important, and they should be equally important to the person you want to be with.

I didn't have much self-love in my first marriage, so I didn't set standards. I allowed myself to be talked to and treated badly for the sake of having a man. I was so afraid of being alone that I let myself be disrespected in many ways. My first husband cheated and verbally tore me down. It caused me to not treat him well. I wasn't a supportive and faithful wife. Because I lacked what I needed from him, which caused me to cheat as well and be disrespectful. I would club every weekend, drink, hang out with my friends, and sleep with other men. At the time, I didn't know I was trying to fill a void and that I didn't love myself; I hadn't dealt with my issues. Also, we were so young and naive: when my first husband would cheat or mistreat me, I felt I should return the favor thinking that this would restore balance in the relationship, but this vengeful behavior only served to hurt us further. When I was with other men, they would make me feel wanted and comfortable with being vulnerable. Since I could not express this with my husband at the time, I fell into the trap. It felt so good to be touched and paid attention to that I got to a point where I didn't care how he felt. I just wanted to feel good and be needed. After realizing sex, booze, and partying couldn't help me, I became tired of the lack of honesty and trust and decided I wanted to work on myself and my marriage. I started visiting another church that my mom was attending, and the pastor gave sermons that spoke directly to my heart and the marital struggles I was facing. He spoke about loving yourself and being happy. He caused me to believe that true fulfillment can happen. I decided that it was time to fully give my life over to God and do things right. I started changing how I looked at myself and how I treated my first husband.

As time went on, I started seeing myself in whole new way and began to believe that I was beautiful, worthy, and special. As I changed my outlook about myself, I began to believe that I was valuable and deserving of happiness. I changed the way I saw life. I changed the way I saw others. I changed the way I saw everything around me.

Adopting a positive outlook slowly removed the negative. People were saying things about me that I didn't believe because they were positive. I wasn't used to people viewing me in a positive way. People usually didn't notice me. As I grew more confident, I made little changes that reflected my renewed sense of self: changed my hair, changed how I dressed, started walking with my head up, and smiled more as my life started getting better. I now knew how important I was to God, myself, and others. My faith in God and myself helped me stay strong for the changes in my marriage that were to come.

Chapter 10: Surviving Breakups / Divorce

Relationships require work. You have someone that you are attracted to and want to be with, so you must do the work to keep them. Often times, it doesn't work that way. Breakups happen for a variety of reasons. Whether you end it, or your partner does, there will be some type of healing that has to happen so you can move forward. Being honest with yourself about the pain is the first step on the road to recovery.

Don't be ashamed to say how separation from your significant other makes you feel. Keep it real with yourself. Let yourself go through the process of healing after the end. No matter what anyone feels, you must make sure that you are prepared to move on.

I thought I found my true love at the age of 16. I got with this guy, and he was so different from the boys I knew so I thought he was the one for me. We had two children together and decided to get married at the age of 19. During the marriage, we were both so immature that we damaged and mistreated each other for most of our marriage. We both cheated on each other, and I was clubbing with my friends. We constantly separated due to the major issues.

We didn't know how to navigate through the woes of marriage. We just knew how to fight so that we could save ourselves individually and not as a whole. We didn't care what we said or did to each other. It was every man for him or herself.

Most people get married with no thought that it will end. We walk down the aisle with the intent to be together forever. Some make the mistake of not looking beyond the ceremony. We don't think about how life would really be for the long haul. This is largely due to both parties not being on the same page when it comes to dedication. One person may be ready for everything life will do to challenge the relationship and be prepared to fight. Unfortunately, the other person may not feel the same. They may not care to work it out or change.

When I became pregnant with our third child, I decided to start changing my ways. However, after the birth of our third daughter, my husband told me he didn't want to be with me anymore. He wanted to be with another woman. I was devastated. I had three children with this man, and I didn't understand why he didn't love me and want to be with me. On top of postpartum depression, I also suffered because yet another man in my life wanted to leave me. Afterwards, I gave my life fully over to God, left my childhood church to join another church, and connected with God on a deeper level. I wanted to be a better wife and mother, so I became closer to God and asked God to guide me. As I grew closer to God by reading the Bible, attending church, and talking to others, I gained wise counsel and began to understand who I was more. I knew I deserved more from my life and marriage. First, I had to treat myself better and believe in who God created me to be. I even got my husband to attend church. It seemed like things were going on the right track. Unfortunately, that wasn't the case.

My husband continued to step out on the marriage, and after I gave birth to our fourth child, I decided I was done and started looking for another place to stay. After a big altercation, that almost ended in violence, I left. I moved in with my mom until I found a place. Later, my husband and I decided to work on our marriage again, but this time I was so secure in who I was that I wasn't taking any mess from him. I refused to move back in with him because I didn't want to risk not having a place to live if our relationship didn't work and wanted to keep my independence. Also, he had another child from another woman, so I wasn't letting him off the hook easily. We went to counseling to repair what we could of our relationship and try to become better spouses to each other. I prayed to God that if he didn't want me to stay in the marriage, he would show me proof that I needed to end it. God gave me exactly what I asked for when I found out my husband was still trying to be with the mother of his other child. That day, I decided that I was completely done, and because of God and my new self-confidence, I was at peace with my decision.

It's true what they say: when a woman is fed up, there is nothing you can do about it. I was ready to release all the heartache, pain, uncertainty, and insecurity, so I could start my life over. I had to wrap my mind around being single again and doing it as a mother. I wasn't sure how I was going to pull it off, but I knew that I refused to drag me and my kids through the turmoil of my marriage any longer.

When you think about ending a marriage, make sure you try all avenues possible before making your final choice. Don't make decisions out of emotions or temporary situations; Divorce is a permanent decision. Marriage is a sacred and beautiful thing, so don't give up if there's hope. Don't allow stubbornness, egos, or another person to get in the way. Protect your marriage until you have absolute certainty it's over. You don't want to leave with "what ifs."

After our divorce was finalized, it hit me. I was single with four small children. I had no idea what I was going to do and started feeling a little lost. How was I going to raise healthy children in my broken state? How would I heal while trying to be the greatest mother I could be for them? Although I was still hurting, I knew I made the best decision for my children by leaving my husband, but I did not intend them to be separated from him. They would still have an open relationship with their father. No matter what, my goal was not to come between them. I knew how important it was to let them have that connection. My own experience with my biological father caused me to want to ensure they had a close bond with their dad.

Divorce can have so many different effects: it can send you through extreme highs and extreme lows. God spoke to me clearly and said for me not to date for a year, so I can get myself together. He said not to worry about what someone is doing or has done and just to focus on me. I needed to make sure I was completely healed because I didn't want to carry any of my baggage over to a new relationship. I got into the Word of God, prayer, and church attendance very heavily. I focused on my growth spiritually, mentally, and emotionally. The issues that I had were given to God, one by one, because I refused to stay broken and lost. I obtained mentors that helped me daily, and my friends and family were a huge support system. It was also important that I was always upfront about how I was feeling. Too often, we hold onto resentment and are scared to release emotions out of fear of others' responses. Holding onto those destructive emotions will only make it worse and harder to release. The goal is to be happy, healthy and whole for the rest of your life, not just for the moment and not just to look good in front of others. You want to see evidence of progress in every area of your life every single day.

Chapter 11: Recognizing True Love

When I got divorced, I walked into the world of the unknown. I didn't know what was next. I didn't know if I would ever achieve true happiness. I didn't know if I would ever become whole. I didn't know if I would ever find true love. I didn't know how life would pan out for me. I didn't know if my kids would survive such a drastic change in their little lives. All I knew was that I only had God to depend on now. I had to start over from scratch.

I moved out of the house that my (now) ex-husband and I shared together into a low-income apartment. I had nothing but my kids and our clothes. My mom furnished my apartment with pieces from her home, thrift stores, and garage sales. Now, my entire focus was to raise my children into healthy individuals as much as possible with the challenge of being a single mom. I had to mourn the end of marriage while making sure they felt loved. I had to push myself to be happy although I saw nothing but sadness around me. I made peace with the decision I made, but it was still tough to deal with. Where was I going to end up? Would anyone ever love me? Would anyone want a twenty-something-year-old mother of four children? I had no answers, so I put all of my faith into God and just let life flow. I surrounded myself with people that breathed life into me with their support and prayed like my life depended on it. My desire was to never go through what I went through in my marriage again.

No matter what my ex-husband did to me, I had to understand that it takes two to end a relationship. I took my focus off of the fact that as soon as we divorced he moved in with the woman he had a baby with and, soon afterwards, they were married. That sent me into another whirlwind of emotions. It baffled me to hear from my kids that the very woman that was part of the demise of our marriage was who he ended up marrying. I didn't blame her for the end, but it was still a tough situation to handle. During this process of healing, I was hit with emotional blows left and right, but I couldn't give up. I had to make it through so my babies would have a chance. There was no way I was going to allow them to endure heartache from the divorce, so I continued to grow mentally and spiritually. I wanted to make sure the next time I loved someone it would be through God's eyes and not my flesh.

Almost a year after my divorce, I started dating; I felt I was ready. However, I made a commitment beforehand to not give my body away to anyone until I was married. I begin hanging out with guys from time-to-time, talking on the phone and other simple ways of spending time and communicating. I didn't want to become too serious with anyone because I knew that when I love I love hard. I wanted to be very careful to not fall quick and to be a great example of healthy love to my kids. Eventually the "keeping myself until marriage" commitment didn't last. My flesh got the best of me, and I slept with someone who I thought wouldn't hurt me because we were friends but that turned out to not be the case. After dealing with that pain, I didn't get serious with anyone else. I was too scared of getting hurt again and I just remained friends with other men. I ended up sleeping with two guys just for fun and to convince myself I could do it without attachments. My convictions got the best of me and I, again, decided not to sleep with anyone else.

Later, I met a man online. He was everything I ever dreamed of. The way he talked to me was so attractive that I agreed to meet him. After we met, we quickly became inseparable, and we talked on the phone constantly, and he came to my house almost daily. It got to the point where he was practically living with me. I knew I had found the one. He was a Jesus freak like me, he made sure everyone always knew how he felt about me, and he treated me like a queen. As time went on, we visited each other's churches, met each other's pastors, families, and kids. We believed we were in love and were going to be married. As time went on, I started to notice that he had some possessive tendencies. It became too much for me to deal with, so I ended it, yet I was surprised by how I felt. I usually hurt deeply after break ups, but that wasn't the case this time. It felt like a weight had been lifted. I had become so confident in who I was and what I deserved that the separation didn't take me out. I knew that if I had to end this relationship, God had something greater for me. I put my trust in Him knowing He would look out for me.

Later on, I started giving rides to a man from my church. I was never attracted to him, and even though my sister, my mom, and one of my friends wanted us to date, I refused. He wasn't my type at all. However, as I gave him more rides, we got to know each other more. He initiated conversations that revealed his frame of mind. I was shocked almost every time we had a conversation because he didn't seem like the kind of man that would think the way he did. In some ways we were alike. We both loved all kinds of music and thought about life in the long-term and not just for the moment. However, his outlook on the world was different from mine in a good way. I was learning so much about things I never would've thought about before. He had knowledge in areas, like nature and history, that I didn't. He was broadening my knowledge and experience.

Over time, I slowly became attracted to his intellect. Initially, he wasn't attracted to me either, so when our feelings started to change, we didn't know what to do with them. We started to entertain the thought of dating. Even though we second guessed it most of the time, we couldn't deny what was happening between us. We began to date secretly because we didn't want anyone else involved in case it didn't work out.

Towards the beginning of our relationship, my biological father died. Even though the relationship between myself and my biological father was not a good one, I grieved for him. The man I was seeing was there for me every step of the way. He let me cry, talk, and feel however I wanted. He helped me through the hectic process of coming to terms with the fact that my biological father wasn't going to be around to give me the love I wanted. That opportunity of having a loving father was gone forever. So, the more the man I was dating was there, the more we talked, the more we went out, and the more time we spent together. Eventually, I realized he was the one.

He was always honest with me about how he felt. We both let each other know our heart's desires. I wanted to be with someone who had kids, but he didn't have kids. He wanted someone without kids, but I had kids. He didn't want to be married at the time, but I only desired to date someone that I would one day marry. Later, he felt the family life was too much for him, and out of respect, we agreed to part ways. It was so difficult to do because I knew that we were supposed to be together. I was so hurt and couldn't understand why it had to be that way. However, I had to respect his desires and believe one day he would want the same life I wanted. Later, we got back together but he still didn't want to get married. We were having sex occasionally, and because I was constantly conflicted, I told him I couldn't live like this anymore unless he decided to marry me. Because he wasn't ready, we broke up again.

I knew that our relationship was permanently over this time, and I was extremely hurt. I knew God told me that we were supposed to be together but what was I supposed to do? I couldn't make him marry me. I couldn't stay in a relationship that wasn't going where I wanted it to go. I had to deal with the tough situation of still loving a man that didn't have the same desires I had and seeing him all the time since we attended the same church. I had to work through the pain publicly without anyone knowing. At this time, our friends and family knew we were dating but no one knew we broke up. I wanted to handle it privately, so no one could influence me or try to get involved. I worked on moving on daily and dealt with the pain of not being with someone I knew God ordained for me. I knew I couldn't dwell in that space for too long, so I quickly tried to recover.

    Later, my ex-boyfriend started getting in contact with me. I was so numb to him at this point that I didn't care for anything he had to say. One day we had a conversation and he told me how much he cared about me and really wanted to be with me. I wasn't really moved by it being that this was all said before. I let him know that I didn't want to be in a relationship unless it was going towards marriage. He would have to show me that he was serious about us having a life together before I considered being with him. When I knew that he was serious about committing to me, we got back together.

Chapter 12: Happily Ever After

Love isn't a fairytale, but you can definitely obtain happily ever after. Everyday won't be peaches and cream. Your mate won't be 100 percent perfect. Your life isn't going to change magically when you get married. Marriage is constant work. It's not easy to adjust to nor to maintain. You must make sure that when you make the decision to marry you are up for the fight.

Marriage is a partnership: it's two people coming together with the intent to build a life together and continuously be there for one another. It's accepting flaws and all. It's knowing that you won't get everything you want out of it, but you will get everything you need. After I decided to take my ex-boyfriend back, I gave him a deadline for when I wanted to be engaged. He promised he would make it happen.

That day came and went. We had some bumps that caused it not to happen, but I was becoming restless. He was living with me, and I wanted to get married soon so that I wouldn't continue to disappoint God and I didn't want to live the wrong example in front of my kids. Although we were abstaining from sex, I still wanted to make it official.

Some months later, I had become fed up. I wanted to be done with the relationship. I couldn't deal with waiting anymore. I called my closest friends and let them know I was over it and I was leaving him. They tried to convince me to stay, so they took me out and had a "come to Jesus" moment with me. They got me to realize what I had and what I could potentially lose. Unbeknownst to me, they already knew he was planning to propose. So, without spilling the beans, they got me to be a little more patient.

A couple of months later one of my best friends told me she decided to have a celebration for her deceased father. My boyfriend and I went to a restaurant to meet her and some other people. We got to the restaurant and I noticed that it was all the people close to me there and none of them knew her father. I started to figure out that this event was for me. After we ate, a waiter brought out a plate with a folded napkin on it. He gave it to my boyfriend who then turned and got on one knee to propose to me. I kind of already knew what was about to happen so I wasn't too shocked, but I was absolutely excited. But I also knew that the work didn't end here, and I was more than ready to dedicate myself to having a healthy marriage.

Before we got engaged, I talked constantly with my kids about the change that would come. They are close to their biological father, so I knew it would be tough. Kids want their parents to be together, so my boyfriend and I always tried to be very understanding. I got a counselor to come to our home on a regular basis to help them cope. We also had a meeting with our bishop to discuss the matter. I never wanted them to feel like I was choosing someone else over them. A part of that process was helping the children to understand that I had a right to be happy and that I was not getting back together with their father. While this was difficult for them to understand, they loved my boyfriend, so they were extremely happy when he told them what was about to happen. Eventually, my children accepted the change and created a celebration for us when we got engaged. It was so important for me to know that they were happy and accepting of the changes that our whole family was about to go through together. We immediately started planning the wedding, so we didn't have to wait too long. I wanted to be in the will of God and to be a great model for my kids. Eight months later, we were married.

Chapter 13: Learning Your Mate

After the wedding, after everyone has gone home and you have come back from your honeymoon, you go right into starting your life with your significant other. Even though my husband and I lived together before we said, "I do," I don't recommend living together before marriage due to my beliefs and the temptation that comes with it. Learning your mate before marriage so you are not blindsided by their actions or beliefs is important to being mature and calm when dealing with obstacles and conflicts you may encounter. You also want to make sure you're paying close attention to telltale signs of behaviors that could potentially become a problem. You must get a handle on them before marriage because afterwards they will only get worse.

You will probably have some of your biggest disagreements before you get married. Don't worry; that is good to have. You want to be able to fix the bigger issues before you make such a major commitment. That's not to say that you won't have issues after marriage, but you'll understand where your spouse stands on the issues you know you're not willing to compromise on. A marriage without problems is called a fairytale, and you want to live in reality.

Once you share each other's space after marriage, whether you already lived together or not, there are another set of adjustments you need to learn. Contrary to belief, living together before you are married is not the same as living together after you're married. When you get married, the option to leave is much harder and shouldn't be a thought at all. After you make those vows to one another, your goal is to uphold them as much as possible. You should be aiming to please your mate daily and to ensure that your relationship is happy, healthy and whole: learning what makes that person upset, sad, disappointed, frustrated, happy, laugh, feel loved, etc. Living and making decisions together show how you and your partner handle different points of views, personalities, and compromise. Ego, pride, and personal agenda can't reside in your process of decision making. You must have a clear agenda when making decisions and learning to cohabitate. You must keep the other person's interest in mind, and the decisions you both make have to end up benefiting you both.

When addressing your mate, make sure your tone and attitude isn't offensive. If you are on your guard with your spouse, this can make them defensive and cause them to come back with a defense mechanism to ward off the offense they feel. Now you are at each other's throats saying and doing things that shouldn't be said or done. There is no such thing as a one-person team: this is a unit. In order for the unit to work, you've got to be able to come together with your spouse. Marriage is like a boxing match only you are not fighting against each other. You are in each other's corner as you fight all the insecurities, people, and struggles that attempt to come in between you two.

When you're doing whatever is needed to make your relationship work, this is where God comes in. He should be the head of your marriage. You want to follow Him as you build this life together. The enemy knows what to do to cause discord, so you must be prepared for the blows. As a team, one is throwing the punches and the other is on the sidelines cheering and taking care of the wounded partner. Often times, you will have to fight together. Either way, God is standing in the gap to handle anything that could cause major damage.

You still have to be mindful of the small troubles that can grow into big troubles. You don't want to be so blinded or busy with life that you ignore the issues that can blow your marriage up. Do constant evaluations of yourself and the relationship as a whole. Be aware of the steps you can take to do better. Making sure you have a mentor, both individually and collectively, is helpful. It's always great to have someone else's view on your relationship to help identify the issues and resolutions you and your partner may not be able to see.

Read the word and pray together. These practices will guarantee that God will handle whatever you need. Make sure you listen to each other and show each other that you are constantly taking into account what the other person is saying. If your mate has a desire or a dream, try to help them make it happen. Don't ever lose sight of why you love this person, and don't forget how they make you feel. As long as you honor, respect, communicate, and be honest to each other, your relationship will work out better than you can imagine.

CONCLUSION

Relationships can be tough, but they are manageable. You can be successful with them if your goal is always to be happy, healthy, and whole. Now that you have read this book, you will have the tools to go out and create awesome relationships. Every relationship won't be exactly how you want it to be, but it's up to you to utilize what you have learned to make a real effort. It takes a lot of work to get a connection in good shape after years of damage. Remember that nothing happens overnight or without hard work. If you really want a healthy connection with someone, you must get to the root of what's making the relationship unhealthy and pull it out. Deal with the tough conflicts that no one wants to talk about. Face your fears and demons. Building and maintaining relationships comes with a price. There are sacrifices and compromises you will have to make. You must pay that price to get what you ultimately want. It's not going to just happen because you want it to. Wishful thinking will keep you stuck.

I pray that my story and advice helps every person that reads this book. Your story may not be just like mine but pay attention to the parts that speak to you. There are no guarantees in life, but I believe that as long as you trust God and put in the work, He will make what you deserve happen. Now, go live a life that is happy, healthy, and whole.

www.ingramcontent.com/pod-product-compliance
Lightning Source LLC
Chambersburg PA
CBHW071532080526
44588CB00011B/1653